Hello Spanish!

Spanish-English
Picture Dictionary

Índice   Contents

numbers

1 uno **oono** *one*

2 dos **doss** *two*

3 tres **trayss** *three*

4 cuatro **kwa-tro** *four*

5 cinco **thin-ko** *five*

6 seis **sayss** *six*

7 siete **see-eh-teh** *seven*

8 ocho **och-o** *eight*

9 nueve **noo-eh-beh** *nine*

10 diez **dee-eth** *ten*

11 once **on-theh** *eleven*

12 doce **doth-eh** *twelve*

13 trece **treth-eh** *thirteen*

14 catorce **kat-or-theh** *fourteen*

15 quince **kin-theh** *fifteen*

16 dieciséis **dee-eh-thee-sayss** *sixteen*

17 diecisiete **dee-eh-thee-see-eh-te** *seventeen*

18 dieciocho **dee-eh-thee-och-o** *eighteen*

19 diecinueve **dee-eh-thee-noo-eh-beh** *nineteen*

20 veinte **bay-en-teh** *twenty*

seasons

la primavera
la preema-vaira
spring

el verano
el bairah-no
summer

el otoño
el oton-yo
autumn

el invierno
el enbee-yair-no
winter

365 el año
el an-yo
year

12 los meses
loss meh-sess
months

enero	febrero	marzo	abril
en-airo	**feb-rairo**	**martho**	**abreel**
January	*February*	*March*	*April*
mayo	junio	julio	agosto
mah-yo	**hoon-yo**	**hool-yo**	**ah-gos-toh**
May	*June*	*July*	*August*
septiembre	octubre	noviembre	diciembre
sept-yem-breh	**ok-too-breh**	**nob-yem-breh**	**deeth-yem-breh**
September	*October*	*November*	*December*

at home

el tejado
el teh-<u>had</u>-o *roof*

el garaje
el gar-<u>rah</u>-heh *garage*

la chimenea
la chimen-<u>eh</u>-ya *chimney*

la ventana
la ben<u>tah</u>-na *window*

la puerta
la <u>pwair</u>-ta *door*

el cubo de basura
el <u>koob</u>-o deh bas-<u>oo</u>-ra
bin

la escalera
la eska<u>lair</u>-a *ladder*

la pelota
la pel<u>ot</u>-a *ball*

el camino
el kam-<u>een</u>-o *path*

in the garden

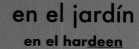

el nido
el <u>nee</u>-do *nest*

el árbol
el <u>ar</u>-bol *tree*

la valla
la <u>bah</u>-ya *fence*

la manguera
la man-<u>gair</u>-a *hose pipe*

el césped
el <u>thess</u>-ped *grass*

el gusano
el goo-<u>san</u>-o *worm*

la flor
la <u>flor</u> *flower*

la puerta de la verja
la <u>pwair</u>ta deh la <u>bair</u>-ha
gate

el seto
el <u>se</u>-to *hedge*

kitchen

la cocina
la kotheena

la nevera
la neh-baira *fridge*

el cuchillo
el koochee-yo *knife*

el horno
el or-no *oven*

el armario
el ar-mah-reeyo *cupboard*

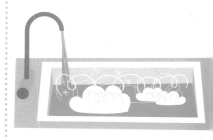

la cuchara
la koochah-ra *spoon*

el fregadero
el fregga-dair-o *sink*

el tenedor
el teneh-dor *fork*

la taza de té
la tath-a deh teh *cup of tea*

el café
el ka-feh *coffee*

living room

el teléfono
el teh-leh-fono *telephone*

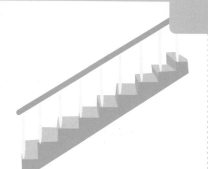

la escalera
la eskal-aira *stairs*

el sofá
el soh-fa *sofa*

el cojín
el koheen *cushion*

la televisión
la teh-leh-vis-yon *television*

la consola
la kon-sol-a *games console*

el techo
el teh-cho *ceiling*

el sillón
el see-yon *armchair*

el suelo
el sweh-lo *floor*

bathroom

la ducha
la <u>doo</u>cha *shower*

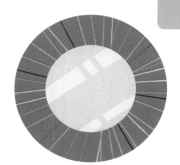

el espejo
el es<u>peh</u>-ho *mirror*

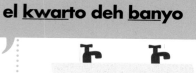

el lavabo
el la<u>bah</u>-bo *sink*

la pasta de dientes
la <u>pa</u>sta deh dee-<u>yen</u>tes
toothpaste

el jabón
el hab<u>bon</u> *soap*

el inodoro
el eeno-<u>dor</u>-o *toilet*

el cepillo de dientes
el the<u>pee</u>-yo deh dee-<u>yen</u>tes
toothbrush

la toalla
la toh-<u>wah</u>-ya *towel*

la bañera
la ban<u>yair</u>-a *bath*

bedroom

la cómoda
la <u>kom</u>-oda *chest of drawers*

el armario
el ar-<u>mah</u>-reeyo *wardrobe*

la cama
la <u>kah</u>-ma *bed*

el póster
el <u>pos</u>tair *poster*

la muñeca
la moon-<u>yeh</u>-ka *doll*

el oso de peluche
el oso deh pel<u>oo</u>cheh
teddy bear

las cortinas
lass kor-<u>teen</u>-ass *curtains*

la alfombra
la al-<u>fom</u>-bra *rug*

el despertador
el despairta-<u>dor</u> *alarm clock*

town

la ciudad
la thee-oo-<u>thad</u>

la iglesia
la eeg-<u>lay</u>-seeya *church*

la sinagoga
la seena-<u>gog</u>-a *synagogue*

el cine
el <u>thee</u>-neh *cinema*

la mezquita
la meth-<u>keeta</u> *mosque*

la estación de tren
la es-stath-<u>yon</u> deh tren
train station

la oficina de correos
la ofee<u>thee</u>-na deh korr-<u>eh</u>-os
post office

el ayuntamiento
el ah-yoontam-<u>yen</u>to *town hall*

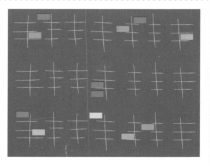

el aparcamiento
el ah-parkam-<u>yen</u>to *car park*

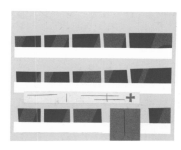

el hospital
el osspee-<u>tal</u> *hospital*

vehicles

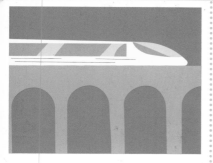

el tren
el tren *train*

la moto
la <u>moh</u>-toh *motorbike*

el avión
el abee-<u>on</u> *aeroplane*

el camión de bomberos
el kamee-<u>on</u> deh bomb<u>air</u>-oss
fire engine

el coche de policía
el <u>ko</u>cheh deh polee<u>thee</u>-ya
police car

la ambulancia
la amboo-<u>lan</u>-theea
ambulance

el coche
el <u>ko</u>cheh *car*

el taxi
el <u>tax</u>-ee *taxi*

el autobús
el ah-oo-to<u>booss</u> *bus*

11

supermarket

la pescadería
la peskadair-ee-a
fishmonger

la carnicería
la karneethair-ee-a
butcher

el dinero
el dee-nairo   *money*

el carro
el kar-o
shopping trolley

la cesta
la thess-ta
shopping basket

la bolsa de la compra
la bolsa deh la kompra
shopping bag

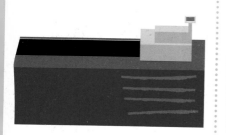

la caja
la kah-ha *till*

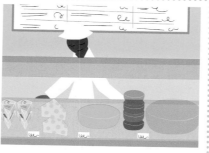

el quesero
el keh-sairo   *cheesemonger*

la panadería
la panadair-ee-a
bakery

shopping

la leche
la <u>leh</u>-cheh *milk*

el arroz
el ar-<u>roth</u> *rice*

los huevos
loss <u>hway</u>-boss *eggs*

la carne
la <u>kar</u>-neh *meat*

el queso
el <u>keh</u>-soh *cheese*

la mantequilla
la manteh-<u>kee</u>-ya *butter*

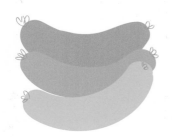

las salchichas
lass salch<u>ee</u>-chass *sausages*

la pasta
la <u>pas</u>-tah *pasta*

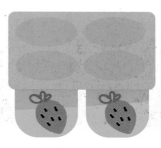

el yogur
el yog-<u>oor</u> *yoghurt*

13

fruit

la manzana
la man-<u>thah</u>-na *apple*

el albaricoque
el albaree-<u>kok</u>-eh *apricot*

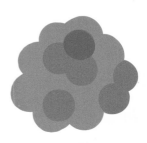

la naranja
la nah-<u>ran</u>-hah *orange*

la uva
la <u>ooba</u> *grapes*

la fresa
la <u>fray</u>-sa *strawberry*

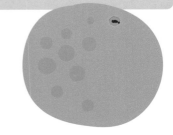

la frambuesa
la fram-<u>bway</u>-sa *raspberry*

el plátano
el <u>plah</u>-tan-oh *banana*

la pera
la <u>pair</u>-a *pear*

el melocotón
el meh-lo-<u>koton</u> *peach*

14

vegetables

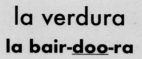

el tomate
el tom-ah-teh *tomato*

el brócoli
el brok-olee *broccoli*

la zanahoria
la thanah-or-ee-a *carrot*

las judías verdes
lass hoo-dee-ass bair-dess
green beans

el calabacín
el kalah-bah-theen *courgette*

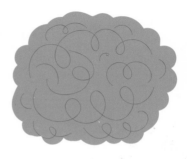

el apio
el ah-pee-o *celery*

el maíz
el mah-eess *sweetcorn*

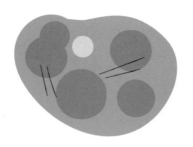

la patata
la pah-tah-ta *potato*

la lechuga
la letchoo-gah *lettuce*

park

el lago
el lah-go *lake*

el puente
el pwen-te *bridge*

el pato
el pat-o *duck*

el banco
el ban-ko *bench*

el cisne
el theesneh *swan*

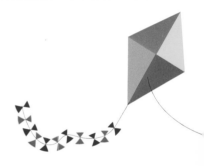

la cometa
la komeh-ta *kite*

el río
el ree-oh *river*

el perro
el peh-ro *dog*

el helado
el el-lah-do *ice cream*

sport

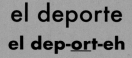

el deporte
el dep-<u>ort</u>-eh

el monopatín
el mono-pat-<u>een</u> *skateboard*

el fútbol
el <u>foot</u>-bol *football*

el tenis
el <u>ten</u>-eess *tennis*

la carrera
la kah-<u>raira</u> *running*

el baloncesto
el balon-<u>thess</u>-sto
basketball

el béisbol
el <u>base</u>-bol *baseball*

la bicicleta
la bee-thee-<u>klet</u>-a *bicycle*

el rugby
el <u>roog</u>-bee *rugby*

la gimnasia
la hin-<u>ah</u>-seea *gymnastics*

17

in the forest

el ratón
el rat-on *mouse*

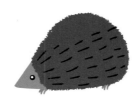

el erizo
el air-ee-tho *hedgehog*

el búho
el boo-ho *owl*

la oruga
la oroo-ga *caterpillar*

el zorro
el thor-roh *fox*

la ardilla
la ardee-ya *squirrel*

el pájaro
el pa-hah-roh *bird*

el ciervo
el thee-air-bo *deer*

el escarabajo
el eskah-rah-bah-ho *beetle*

weather

calor
ka-lor *hot*

frío
free-o *cold*

la nube
la noo-beh *cloud*

el sol
el sol *sun*

el viento
el bee-en-toh *wind*

la niebla
la nee-aybla *fog*

la tormenta
la tormen-tah *storm*

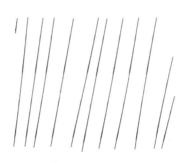

la lluvia
la yoo-beea *rain*

la nieve
la nee-eh-beh *snow*

opposites

encima
enth-<u>ee</u>-ma *on top*

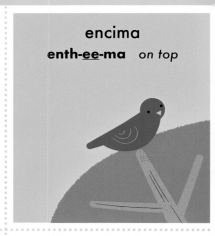

grande
<u>gran</u>-deh *big*

pequeño/pequeña
pek-<u>en</u>-yo/pek-<u>en</u>-ya *small*

arriba
a<u>ree</u>-ba *high up*

dentro
<u>dentro</u> *inside*

debajo
de<u>bah</u>-ho *under*

abajo
<u>abah</u>-ho *low down*

fuera
fw<u>aira</u> *outside*

rápido/rápida
ra<u>peedo</u>/ra<u>peeda</u> *fast*

viejo/vieja
bee-<u>eh</u>-ho/bee-<u>eh</u>-ha *old*

desordenado/desordenada
des-orde<u>nad</u>-o/des-orde<u>nad</u>-a
messy

ordenado/ordenada
orde<u>nad</u>-o/orde<u>nad</u>-a
tidy

joven
<u>ho</u>ven *young*

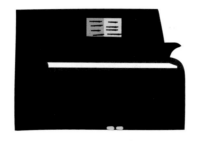

pesado/pesada
pes-<u>ad</u>-o/pes-<u>ad</u>-a *heavy*

ligero/ligera
lee-<u>hair</u>-o/lee-<u>hair</u>-a *light*

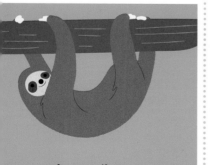

lento/lenta
<u>lento</u>/<u>lenta</u> *slow*

sucio/sucia
<u>soo</u>-theeo/<u>soo</u>-theea *dirty*

limpio/limpia
<u>leem</u>-peeo/ <u>leem</u>-peea *clean*

shapes

el rectángulo
el rekt<u>an</u>-goolo *rectangle*

el rombo
el <u>rombo</u> *rhombus*

la estrella
la ess<u>tray</u>-a *star*

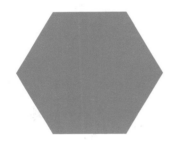

el hexágono
el ex-<u>ag</u>-ono *hexagon*

el pentágono
el pen-<u>tag</u>-ono *pentagon*

el óvalo
el <u>oh</u>-balo *oval*

el círculo
el <u>theer</u>-koolo *circle*

el triángulo
el tree-<u>an</u>-goolo *triangle*

el cuadrado
el kwah-<u>drad</u>-o *square*

swimming pool

el traje de baño
el tra-heh deh banyo
swimming costume

el gorro de piscina
el goh-ro deh pee-theen-a
swimming cap

las gafas de natación
lass gafass deh natath-yon
swimming goggles

el corcho
el kor-cho *diving board*

el champú
el cham-poo *shampoo*

yo nado
yo nah-do *I am swimming*

el socorrista/la socorrista
el sokor-ee-sta/ la sokor-ee-sta
lifeguard (man/woman)

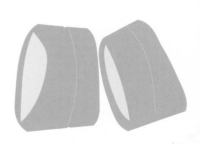

la natación
la natath-yon *swimming*

los manguitos
loss man-gee-toss *armbands*

library

había una vez
ah-bee-ya oona veth
once upon a time

el bibliotecario/
la bibliotecaria
el/la beebleeo-tek-ar-eeo/a *librarian*

el álbum ilustrado
el al-boom eel-ooss-trado
picture book

el cómic
el kom-eek *comic*

la hora del cuento
la or-a del kwen-toh
storytime

el disfraz
el deessfrath *costume*

la estantería
la ess-tantair-ee-a *shelf*

el puf
el poof *beanbag*

el ordenador
el ordenad-dor *computer*

stories

el pirata
el pee-rah-ta *pirate*

el castillo
el kastee-yo *castle*

la sirena
la see-rain-a *fairy*

el hada
el ah-da *fairy*

la bruja
la broo-ha *witch*

el unicornio
el oonee-korn-eeo *unicorn*

la princesa
la preen-thessa *princess*

el caballero
el kaba-yair-o *knight*

el dragón
el drah-gon *dragon*

on my desk

la libreta
la leebr<u>eh</u>-tah *notebook*

la regla
la <u>reh</u>-gla *ruler*

el bolígrafo
el bol-<u>ee</u>-grafo *pen*

el papel
el pap-<u>el</u> *paper*

las pinturas
lass peen-<u>too</u>-rass *paints*

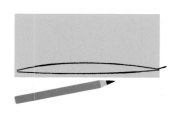

el estuche
el est-<u>oo</u>-cheh *pencil case*

el lápiz de color
el <u>lap</u>-eeth deh kol<u>or</u>
colouring pencil

las tijeras
lass tee-<u>hair</u>-ass *scissors*

el pegamento
el pega-<u>men</u>to *glue*

classroom

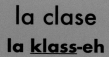

el maestro
el mah-<u>eh</u>-stro *teacher (man)*

la maestra
la mah-<u>eh</u>-stra *teacher (woman)*

el reloj
el rel<u>okh</u> *clock*

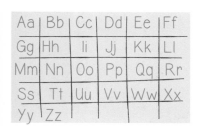

el abecedario
el abeh-theh-<u>dar</u>-eeo
alphabet

el libro
el <u>lee</u>bro *book*

la silla
la <u>see</u>-ya *chair*

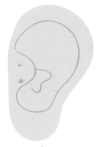

¡escuchad!
es-<u>koo</u>-chad *listen!*

¡mirad!
<u>mee</u>-rad *look!*

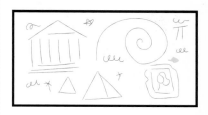

la pizarra
la peeth-<u>ah</u>-rah
whiteboard

body

la nariz
la na<u>reeth</u> *nose*

el brazo
el <u>brah</u>-tho *arm*

la cabeza
la ka<u>beh</u>-tha *head*

la boca
la <u>bok</u>ka *mouth*

la pierna
la pee-<u>yair</u>na *leg*

la mano
la <u>mah</u>-no *hand*

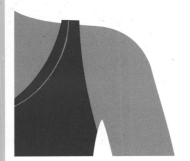

el hombro
el <u>om</u>bro *shoulder*

las rodillas
lass rod-<u>ee</u>-yass *knees*

el pie
el pee-<u>yeh</u> *foot*

el cuerpo
el **kwair**-po

los ojos
loss <u>oh</u>-hos *eyes*

la oreja
la <u>oreh</u>-ha *ear*

el codo
el <u>kodo</u> *elbow*

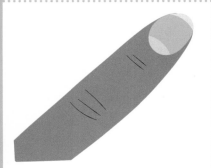

el dedo
el <u>dehdo</u> *finger*

los dedos del pie
loss <u>dehdos</u> del pee-<u>eh</u> *toes*

el pecho
el <u>peh</u>-cho *chest*

los labios
loss <u>lab</u>-eeyoss *lips*

la espalda
la <u>esspalda</u> *back*

la cara
la <u>kah</u>-ra *face*

29

actions

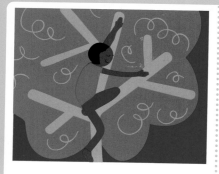

trepar

trep-ar *climbing*

saltar a la comba

sal-tar ah la kom-ba *skipping*

empujar

empoo-har *pushing*

saltar

sal-tar *jumping*

abrazarse

abratharseh *hugging*

estirar

ess-teer-ar *pulling*

correr

koh-rair *running*

lanzar

lan-thar *throwing*

bailar

bah-ee-lar *dancing*

30

playground

la piscina hinchable
la pee-<u>thee</u>-na eench<u>a</u>bleh
paddling pool

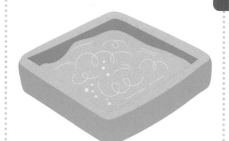

el arenero
el ah-rain-<u>airo</u>   *sandpit*

el carrusel
el <u>karoo</u>-<u>sell</u>   *roundabout*

el balancín
el balan-<u>theen</u>   *see-saw*

el tobogán
el tobo-<u>gan</u>   *slide*

el columpio
el kol-<u>oom</u>-pee-o   *swing*

el pasamanos
el passa-<u>man</u>-oss
climbing frame

el niño
el <u>neen</u>-yo   *boy*

la niña
la <u>neen</u>-ya   *girl*

party

el pastel de cumpleaños
el pas-_tel_ deh koomplay-_an_-yoss
birthday cake

la limonada
la leemo_nah_-da *lemonade*

el polo
el _poh_-lo *ice lolly*

la pizza
la _peet_-za *pizza*

el batido
el ba_teedo_ *milkshake*

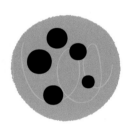

la galleta
la gah-_yeta_ *biscuit*

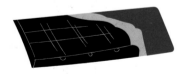

el chocolate
el chokko-_lah_-teh *chocolate*

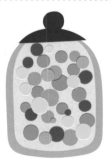

los caramelos
loss kara-_meh_-loss *sweets*

el bocadillo
el boka-_dee_-yo *sandwich*

clothes

la falda
la <u>fal</u>-da *skirt*

el vestido
el best<u>ee</u>do *dress*

el sombrero
el som<u>brai</u>ro *hat*

el abrigo
el ab<u>ree</u>-go *coat*

la camisa
la kah-<u>mee</u>-sa *shirt*

el pijama
el pee<u>hah</u>-ma *pyjamas*

los zapatos
loss tha<u>pat</u>-oss *shoes*

los calcetines
loss kaltheh-<u>tee</u>-ness *socks*

los pantalones
loss pantal<u>on</u>ess *trousers*

ZOO

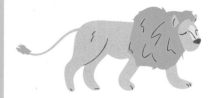

el león
el leh-<u>on</u> *lion*

el hipopótamo
el eepo-<u>pot</u>-amo
hippopotamus

el oso
el <u>osso</u> *bear*

el elefante
el eleh-<u>fan</u>-teh *elephant*

la gacela
la gath-<u>eh</u>-la *gazelle*

la jirafa
la hee-<u>rah</u>-fa *giraffe*

el rinoceronte
el reeno-thair<u>on</u>-teh
rhinoceros

el cocodrilo
el kokko-<u>dree</u>-lo *crocodile*

la serpiente
la sairp-<u>yen</u>-teh *snake*

34

under the sea

el submarinista/
la submarinista
el soob-mareen<u>ee</u>-sta/
la soob-mareen<u>ee</u>-sta
diver (man/woman)

el pulpo
el <u>pool</u>-po   *octopus*

el delfín
el del-<u>feen</u>   *dolphin*

el coral
el k<u>oral</u>   *coral*

el naufragio
el now-<u>frah</u>-hee-o   *shipwreck*

el pez
el peth   *fish*

la ballena
la bah-<u>yay</u>-na   *whale*

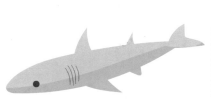

el tiburón
el teeboo-<u>ron</u>   *shark*

la langosta
la lan-<u>goss</u>-ta   *lobster*

beach

el mar
el mar *sea*

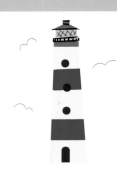

el faro
el fah-ro *lighthouse*

la arena
la ah-reh-na *sand*

la crema solar
la kreh-ma solar *sun cream*

la pala
la pah-la *spade*

la concha
la koncha *shell*

el cubo
el koo-bo *bucket*

la bolsa de playa
la bolsa deh plah-ya
beach bag

el alga marina
el alga mareena *seaweed*

la roca
la rokka rock

la sombrilla
la sombree-ya
beach umbrella

la ola
la oh-la wave

la gaviota
la gab-yota seagull

el cielo
el thee-aylo sky

el barco
el barko boat

la tabla de surf
la tabla deh soorf
surfboard

el castillo de arena
el kastee-yo deh ah-reh-na
sandcastle

el cangrejo
el kangreh-ho crab

farm

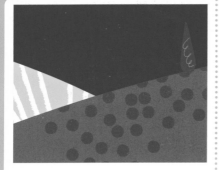

el campo
el <u>kampo</u> *field*

el manzano
el man-<u>than</u>-o *apple tree*

el granero
el gran-<u>airo</u> *barn*

el granjero
el gran-<u>hairo</u> *farmer (man)*

la granjera
la gran-<u>haira</u> *farmer (woman)*

el gallinero
el ga-y<u>een</u>-airo *henhouse*

el heno
el <u>eh</u>-no *hay*

el espantapájaros
el esspanta-<u>pah</u>-haross
scarecrow

el tractor
el trak-<u>tor</u> *tractor*

farm animals

el burro
el <u>buh</u>-roh *donkey*

el caballo
el ka<u>bah</u>-yo *horse*

el gato
el <u>gah</u>-to *cat*

la oveja
la <u>obeh</u>-ha *sheep*

el cerdo
el <u>thair</u>-do *pig*

la vaca
la <u>bah</u>-ka *cow*

el conejo
el kon-<u>eh</u>-ho *rabbit*

la cabra
la <u>kah</u>-bra *goat*

la gallina
la ga-<u>yeen</u>-a *chicken*

describing yourself

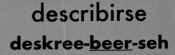

el pelo castaño
el paylo kas-tan-yo *brown hair*

el pelo pelirrojo
el paylo pelee-ro-ho *red hair*

los ojos marrones
loss o-hoss maron-ess
brown eyes

el pelo rubio
el paylo roobeeo *blonde hair*

los ojos azules
loss o-hoss ath-oo-less
blue eyes

el pelo largo
el paylo largo *long hair*

el pelo liso
el paylo leeso *straight hair*

el pelo rizado
el paylo reethado *curly hair*

el pelo corto
el paylo korto *short hair*

family

mi abuelo
mee ab<u>weh</u>-lo
my grandfather

mi abuela
mee ab<u>weh</u>-la
my grandmother

mi tío
mee <u>tee</u>-yo   *my uncle*

mi tía
mee <u>tee</u>-ya   *my aunt*

mi madre
mee <u>mah</u>-dre   *my mother*

mi padre
mee <u>pah</u>-dreh   *my father*

mi hermana
mee air-<u>man</u>-a   *my sister*

mi hermano
mee air-<u>man</u>-o   *my brother*

mis primos/mis primas
mees preemoss/mees preemass
my cousins

41

English to Spanish

A
aeroplane	el avión
alarm clock	el despertador
alphabet	el abecedario
ambulance	la ambulancia
apple	la manzana
apple juice	el zumo de manzana
apple tree	el manzano
apricot	el albaricoque
April	abril
arm	el brazo
armbands	los manguitos
armchair	el sillón
August	agosto
aunt	la tía
autumn	el otoño

B
back	la espalda
bakery	la panadería
ball	la pelota
banana	el plátano
barn	el granero
baseball	el beisbol
basketball	el baloncesto
bath	la bañera
bathroom	el cuarto de baño
beach	la playa
beach umbrella	la sombrilla
beach bag	la bolsa de playa
beanbag	el puf
bear	el oso
bed	la cama
bedroom	la habitación
beetle	el escarabajo
bench	el banco
bicycle	la bicicleta
big	grande
bin	el cubo de basura
bird	el pájaro
birthday cake	el pastel de cumpleaños
biscuit	la galleta
black	negro/a
blue	azul
boat	el barco
body	el cuerpo
book	el libro
boy	el niño
bridge	el puente

C
broccoli	el brócoli
brother	el hermano
brown	marrón
bucket	el cubo
bus	el autobús
butcher	la carnicería
butter	la mantequilla
car	el coche
car park	el aparcamiento
carrot	la zanahoria
castle	el castillo
cat	el gato
caterpillar	la oruga
ceiling	el techo
celery	el apio
chair	la silla
cheese	el queso
cheesemonger	el quesero
chest	el pecho
chest of drawers	la cómoda
chicken	el pollo
chimney	la chimenea
chocolate	el chocolate
church	la iglesia
cinema	el cine
circle	el círculo
classroom	la clase
clean	limpio/a
climb	trepar
climbing frame	el pasamanos
clock	el reloj
clothes	la ropa
cloud	la nube
coat	el abrigo
coffee	el café
cold	frío
colouring pencil	el lápiz de color
colours	los colores
comic	el cómic
computer	el ordenador
coral	el coral
costume	el disfraz
courgette	el calabacín
cousins	los primos
cow	la vaca
crab	el cangrejo
crocodile	el cocodrilo
cup of tea	la taza de té
cupboard	el armario

D
curly	rizado
curtains	los cortinas
cushion	el cojín
dance	bailar
desk	el escritorio
dirty	sucio/a
diver (man)	el submarinista
diver (woman)	la submarinista
diving board	el corcho
dog	el perro
doll	la muñeca
dolphin	el delfín
donkey	el burro
door	la puerta
dragon	el dragón
dress	el vestido
duck	el pato

E
ear	la oreja
eggs	los huevos
eight	ocho
eighteen	dieciocho
elbow	el codo
elephant	el elefante
eleven	once
eyes	los ojos

F
face	la cara
fairy	el hada
family	la familia
farm	la granja
farm animals	los animales de granja
farmer (man)	el granjero
farmer (woman)	la granjera
fast	rápido/a
father	el padre
February	febrero
fence	la valla
field	el campo
fifteen	quince
finger	el dedo
fire engine	el camión de bomberos
fish	el pez
fishmonger	la pescadería
five	cinco
floor	el suelo
flower	la flor
fog	la niebla
foot	el pie

English to Spanish

football	el fútbol
fork	el tenedor
four	cuatro
fourteen	catorce
fox	el zorro
fridge	la nevera
fruit	las frutas
G games console	la consola
garage	el garaje
garden	el jardín
gazelle	la gacela
giraffe	la jirafa
girl	la niña
glue	el pegamento
goat	la cabra
grandfather	el abuelo
grandmother	la abuela
grapes	las uvas
grass	el césped
green	verde
green beans	las judías verdes
gymnastics	la gimnasia
H hand	la mano
hat	el gorro
hay	el heno
head	la cabeza
heavy	pesado/a
hedge	el seto
hedgehog	el erizo
henhouse	el gallinero
hexagon	el hexágono
high up	arriba
hippopotamus	el hipopótamo
horse	el caballo
hose pipe	la manguera
hospital	el hospital
hot	calor
house	la casa
hug	abrazarse
I ice cream	el helado
ice lolly	el polo
inside	dentro
J January	enero
jump	saltar
K kitchen	la cocina
kite	la cometa
knees	las rodillas
knife	el cuchillo
knight	el caballero
L ladder	la escalera
lake	el lago
leg	la pierna
lemonade	la limonada
lettuce	la lechuga
librarian (man)	el bibliotecario
librarian (woman)	la bibliotecaria
library	la biblioteca
lifeguard (man)	el socorrista
lifeguard (woman)	la socorrista
light	ligero/a
lighthouse	el faro
lion	el león
lips	los labios
listen!	¡escuchad!
living room	el salón
lobster	la langosta
look	¡mirad!
long	largo
low down	abajo
M May	mayo
meat	la carne
mermaid	la sirena
messy	desordenado/a
milk	la leche
milkshake	el batido
mirror	el espejo
money	el dinero
month	el mes
mosque	la mezquita
mother	la madre
motorbike	la moto
mouse	el ratón
mouth	la boca
N nest	el nido
nine	nueve
nineteen	diecinueve
nose	la nariz
notebook	el cuaderno
November	noviembre
numbers	los números
O octopus	el pulpo
old	viejo/a
on top	encima
once upon a time	había una vez
one	uno
opposites	los contrarios
orange (colour)	naranja
orange (fruit)	la naranja
outside	fuera
oval	el óvalo
oven	el horno
owl	el búho
P paddling pool	la piscina hinchable
paints	las pinturas
paper	el papel
park	el parque
party	la fiesta
pasta	la pasta
path	el camino
peach	el melocotón
pear	la pera
pen	el bolígrafo
pencil case	el estuche
pentagon	el pentágono
picture book	el álbum ilustrado
pig	el cerdo
pirate	el pirata
pizza	la pizza
playground	el patio
police car	el coche de policía
post office	la oficina de correos
poster	el póster
potato	la patata
princess	la princesa
pull	tirar
purple	morado/a
push	empujar
pyjamas	el pijama
R rabbit	el conejo
rain	la lluvia
raspberry	la frambuesa
rectangle	el rectángulo
red	rojo/a
red (hair)	pelirrojo
rhinoceros	el rinoceronte
rhombus	el rombo
rice	el arroz
river	el río
rock	la roca
roof	el tejado
roundabout	el carrusel
rug	la alfombra
rugby	el rugby

English to Spanish

	English	Spanish
S	ruler	la regla
	run	correr
	running	la carrera
	sand	la arena
	sand castle	el castillo de arena
	sand pit	el arenero
	sandwich	el bocadillo
	sausages	las salchichas
	scarecrow	el espantapájaros
	scissors	las tijeras
	sea	el mar
	seagull	la gaviota
	season	la estación
	seaweed	el alga marina
	see-saw	el balancín
	September	septiembre
	seven	siete
	seventeen	diecisiete
	shampoo	el champú
	shapes	las formas
	shark	el tiburón
	sheep	la oveja
	shelf	la estantería
	shell	la concha
	shipwreck	el naufragio
	shirt	la camiseta
	shoes	los zapatos
	shopping	la compra
	shopping bag	la bolsa de la compra
	shopping basket	la cesta
	shopping trolley	el carro
	shoulder	el hombro
	shower	la ducha
	sink	el fregadero
	sister	la hermana
	six	seis
	sixteen	dieciséis
	skateboard	el monopatín
	skip	saltar a la comba
	skirt	la falda
	sky	el cielo
	slide	el tobogán
	slow	lento/a
	small	pequeño/a
	snake	la serpiente
	snow	la nieve
	soap	el jabón
	socks	los calcetines
	sofa	el sofá
	spade	la pala
	spoon	la cuchara
	sport	el deporte
	spring	la primavera
	square	el cuadrado
	squirrel	la ardilla
	stairs	la escalera
	swim	nadar
	star	la estrella
	stories	los cuentos
	storm	la tormenta
	storytime	la hora de cuento
	straight (hair)	liso/lisa
	strawberry	la fresa
	summer	el verano
	sun	el sol
	suncream	la crema solar
	supermarket	el supermercado
	surfboard	la tabla de surf
	swan	el cisne
	sweetcorn	el maíz
	sweets	los caramelos
	swimming	la natación
	swimming cap	el gorro de piscina
	swimming costume	el traje de baño
	swimming goggles	las gafas de natación
	swimming pool	la piscina
	swing	el columpio
	synagogue	la sinagoga
T	taxi	el taxi
	teacher (woman)	la maestra
	teacher (man)	el maestro
	teddy bear	el oso de peluche
	telephone	el teléfono
	television	la televisión
	ten	diez
	tennis	el tenis
	thirteen	trece
	three	tres
	throw	lanzar
	tidy	ordenado/a
	till	la caja
	toes	los dedos del pie
	toilet	el inodoro
	tomato	la tomate
	toothbrush	el cepillo de dientes
	toothpaste	la pasta de dientes
	towel	la toalla
	town	la ciudad
	town hall	el ayuntamiento
	tractor	el tractor
	train	el tren
	train station	la estación de tren
	tree	el árbol
	triangle	el triángulo
	trousers	los pantalones
	twelve	doce
	twenty	veinte
	two	dos
U	uncle	el tío
	under	debajo
	unicorn	el unicornio
V	vegetables	la verdura
	vehicles	los vehículos
W	wardrobe	el armario
	wave	la ola
	whale	la ballena
	white	blanco/a
	whiteboard	la pizarra
	wind	el viento
	window	la ventana
	winter	el invierno
	witch	la bruja
	worm	el gusano
Y	year	el año
	yellow	amarillo/a
	yoghurt	el yogur
	young	joven
Z	zoo	el zoo

A

Spanish	English
abajo	low down
el abecedario	alphabet
abrazarse	hug
el abrigo	coat
abril	April
la abuela	grandmother
el abuelo	grandfather
el albaricoque	apricot
el álbum ilustrado	picture book
la alfombra	rug
el alga marina	seaweed
amarillo/a	yellow
la ambulancia	ambulance
los animales de granja	farm animals
el año	year
el aparcamiento	car park
el apio	celery
el árbol	tree
la ardilla	squirrel
la arena	sand
el arenero	sand pit
el armario	cupboard
el armario	wardrobe
arriba	high up
el arroz	rice
agosto	August
el autobús	bus
el avión	aeroplane
el ayuntamiento	town hall
azul	blue

B

Spanish	English
bailar	dance
el balancín	see-saw
la ballena	whale
el baloncesto	basketball
el banco	bench
la bañera	bath
el barco	boat
el batido	milkshake
el beisbol	baseball
la biblioteca	library
la bibliotecaria	librarian (woman)
el bibliotecario	librarian (man)
la bicicleta	bicycle
blanco/a	white
la boca	mouth
el bocadillo	sandwich
el bolígrafo	pen

Spanish	English
la bolsa de la compra	shopping bag
la bolsa de playa	beach bag
el brazo	arm
el brócoli	broccoli
la bruja	witch
el búho	owl
el burro	donkey

C

Spanish	English
el caballero	knight
el caballo	horse
la cabeza	head
la cabra	goat
el café	coffee
la caja	till
el calabacín	courgette
los calcetines	socks
calor	hot
la cama	bed
el camino	path
el camión de bomberos	fire engine
la camiseta	shirt
el campo	field
el cangrejo	crab
la cara	face
los caramelos	sweets
la carne	meat
la carnicería	butcher
el carro	shopping trolley
el carrusel	roundabout
la casa	house
el castillo	castle
el castillo de arena	sand castle
catorce	fourteen
el cepillo de dientes	toothbrush
el cerdo	pig
el césped	grass
la cesta	shopping basket
el champú	shampoo
la chimenea	chimney
el chocolate	chocolate
el cielo	sky
cinco	five
el cine	cinema
el círculo	circle
el cisne	swan
la ciudad	town

Spanish	English
la clase	classroom
el coche	car
el coche de policía	police car
la cocina	kitchen
el cocodrilo	crocodile
el codo	elbow
el cojín	cushion
los colores	colours
el columpio	swing
la cometa	kite
el cómic	comic
la cómoda	chest of drawers
la compra	shopping
la concha	shell
el conejo	rabbit
la consola	games console
los contrarios	opposites
el coral	coral
el corcho	diving board
correr	run
la correra	running
los cortinas	curtains
la crema solar	suncream
el cuaderno	notebook
el cuadrado	square
el cuarto de baño	bathroom
cuatro	four
el cubo	bucket
el cubo de basura	bin
la cuchara	spoon
el cuchillo	knife
los cuentos	stories
el cuerpo	body

D

Spanish	English
debajo	under
el dedo	finger
los dedos del pie	toes
el delfín	dolphin
dentro	inside
el deporte	sport
desordenado/a	messy
el despertador	alarm clock
diecinueve	nineteen
dieciocho	eighteen
dieciséis	sixteen
diecisiete	seventeen
diez	ten
el dinero	money
el disfraz	costume
doce	twelve

Spanish	English
E	
la ducha	shower
dos	two
el dragón	dragon
el elefante	elephant
empujar	push
encima	on top
enero	January
el erizo	hedgehog
la escalera	ladder
la escalera	stairs
el escarabajo	beetle
el escritorio	desk
¡escuchad!	listen!
la espalda	back
el espantapájaros	scarecrow
el espejo	mirror
la estación	season
la estación de tren	train station
la estantería	shelf
la estrella	star
el estuche	pencil case
F	
la falda	skirt
la familia	family
el faro	lighthouse
febrero	February
la fiesta	party
la flor	flower
las formas	shapes
la frambuesa	raspberry
el fregadero	sink
la fresa	strawberry
frío	cold
las frutas	fruit
fuera	outside
el fútbol	football
G	
la gacela	gazelle
las gafas de natación	swimming goggles
la galeta	biscuit
el gallinero	henhouse
el garaje	garage
el gato	cat
la gaviota	seagull
la gimnasia	gymnastics
el gorro	hat
el gorro de piscina	swimming cap
grande	big
el granero	barn
la granja	farm
H	
la granjera	farmer (woman)
el granjero	farmer (man)
el gusano	worm
había una vez	once upon a time
la habitación	bedroom
el hada	fairy
el helado	ice cream
el heno	hay
la hermana	sister
el hermano	brother
el hexágono	hexagon
el hipopótamo	hippopotamus
el hombro	shoulder
la hora de cuento	storytime
el horno	oven
el hospital	hospital
los huevos	eggs
I	
la iglesia	church
el inodoro	toilet
invierno	winter
J	
el jabón	soap
el jardín	garden
la jirafa	giraffe
joven	young
las judías verdes	green beans
L	
los labios	lips
el lago	lake
la langosta	lobster
lanzar	throw
el lápiz de color	colouring pencil
largo	long
la leche	milk
la lechuga	lettuce
lento/a	slow
el león	lion
el libro	book
ligero/a	light
la limonada	lemonade
limpio/a	clean
liso/lisa	straight (hair)
la lluvia	rain
M	
la madre	mother
la maestra	teacher (man)
el maestro	teacher (woman)
el maíz	sweetcorn
la manguera	hose pipe
los manguitos	armbands
la mano	hand
la mantequilla	butter
la manzana	apple
el manzano	apple tree
el mar	sea
marrón	brown
mayo	May
el melocotón	peach
el mes	month
la mezquita	mosque
¡mirad!	look
el monopatín	skateboard
morado/a	purple
la moto	motorbike
la muñeca	doll
N	
nadar	swim
naranja	orange (colour)
la naranja	orange (fruit)
la nariz	nose
la natación	swimming
el naufragio	shipwreck
negro/a	black
la nevera	fridge
el nido	nest
la niebla	fog
la nieve	snow
la niña	girl
el niño	boy
noviembre	November
la nube	cloud
nueve	nine
los números	numbers
O	
ocho	eight
la oficina de correos	post office
los ojos	eyes
la ola	wave
once	eleven
ordenado/a	tidy
el ordenador	computer
la oreja	ear
la oruga	caterpillar
el oso de peluche	teddy bear
el oso	bear
el otoño	autumn
el óvalo	oval
la oveja	sheep
P	
el padre	father
el pájaro	bird
la pala	spade
la panadería	bakery

Spanish	English
los pantalones	trousers
el papel	paper
el parque	park
el pasamano	climbing frame
la pasta	pasta
la pasta de dientes	toothpaste
el pastel de cumpleaños	birthday cake
la patata	potato
el patio	playground
el pato	duck
el pecho	chest
el pegamento	glue
pelirrojo	red (hair)
la pelota	ball
el pentágono	pentagon
pequeño/a	small
la pera	pear
el perro	dog
pesado/a	heavy
la pescadería	fishmonger
el pez	fish
el pie	foot
la pierna	leg
el pijama	pyjamas
las pinturas	paints
el pirata	pirate
la piscina	swimming pool
la piscina hinchable	paddling pool
la pizarra	whiteboard
la pizza	pizza
el plátano	banana
la playa	beach
el pollo	chicken
el polo	ice lolly
el póster	poster
primavera	spring
los primos	cousins
la princesa	princess
el puente	bridge
la puerta	door
el puf	beanbag
el pulpo	octopus

Q

Spanish	English
el quesero	cheesemonger
el queso	cheese
quince	fifteen

R

Spanish	English
rápido/a	fast
el ratón	mouse
el rectángulo	rectangle
la regla	ruler
el reloj	clock
el rinoceronte	rhinoceros
el río	river
rizado	curly
la roca	rock
las rodillas	knees
rojo/a	red
el rombo	rhombus
la ropa	clothes
el rugby	rugby

S

Spanish	English
las salchichas	sausages
el salón	living room
saltar	jump
saltar a la comba	skip
seis	six
el seto	hedge
septiembre	September
la serpiente	snake
siete	seven
la silla	chair
el sillón	armchair
la sinagoga	synagogue
la sirena	mermaid
el socorrista	lifeguard (man)
la socorrista	lifeguard (woman)
el sofá	sofa
el sol	sun
la sombrilla	beach umbrella
el submarinista	diver (man)
la submarinista	diver (woman)
sucio/a	dirty
el suelo	floor
el supermercado	supermarket

T

Spanish	English
la tabla de surf	surfboard
el taxi	taxi
la taza de té	cup of tea
el techo	ceiling
el tejado	roof
el teléfono	telephone
la televisión	television
el tenedor	fork
el tenis	tennis
la tía	aunt
el tiburón	shark
las tijeras	scissors
el tío	uncle
tirar	pull
la toalla	towel
el tobogán	slide
la tomate	tomato
la tormenta	storm
el tractor	tractor
el traje de baño	swimming costume
trece	thirteen
el tren	train
trepar	climb
tres	three
el triángulo	triangle

U

Spanish	English
el unicornio	unicorn
uno	one
las uvas	grapes

V

Spanish	English
la vaca	cow
la valla	fence
los vehículos	vehicles
veinte	twenty
la ventana	window
verano	summer
verde	green
la verdura	vegetables
el vestido	dress
viejo/a	old
el viento	wind

Y

Spanish	English
el yogur	yoghurt

Z

Spanish	English
la zanahoria	carrot
los zapatos	shoes
el zoo	zoo
el zorro	fox
el zumo de manzana	apple juice

written by Sam Hutchinson

illustrated by Kim Hankinson

Spanish adviser: Lola Esquina

Published by b small publishing ltd.

www.bsmall.co.uk

Text & Illustrations copyright © b small publishing ltd. 2018

1 2 3 4 5

ISBN 978-1-911509-82-0

Design: Kim Hankinson   Editorial: Emilie Martin & Rachel Thorpe   Production: Madeleine Ehm

Publisher: Sam Hutchinson

Printed in China by WKT Co. Ltd.